JFK

© 2005 Assouline Publishing
601 West 26th Street, 18th floor
New York, NY 10001, USA
Tel.: 212 989-6810   Fax: 212 647-0005
www.assouline.com

Photographs: © 1999 Jacques Lowe and Jacques Lowe Visual Arts Projects Inc.,
except for pages 20-21, 22, and 75.

Color separation: Gravor (Switzerland)
Printed by Grafiche Milani (Italy)

ISBN: 2 84323 773 4

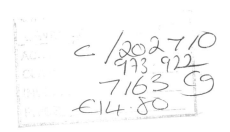
JFK

EXCERPTS FROM IMPORTANT SPEECHES
INTRODUCTION BY JACQUES LOWE

ASSOULINE

i met John Fitzgerald Kennedy for the first time in Hyannis Port, Massachusetts, on a hot day in July 1958. The family patriarch, the ambassador Joseph P. Kennedy, invited me to the Kennedy estate to photograph his eldest son.

Two years earlier, as part of my work as a photojournalist, I had met the ambassador's other son, Robert, and we became friends. I visited Robert several times at his home in McLean, Virginia, where I had ample opportunity to take photographs. Dozens of children, animals, adult women and men would join together in boisterous games of football, stickball, horseback rides, tennis, swimming, and other acts of bravura. It mostly all seemed like joyful chaos. Bobby loved my worked and asked me to shoot a series of photographs to give to his father for his birthday.

I arrived from New York on a Sunday morning with my assistant. I had never met the head of the family, even though he had called me the night of his birthday to congratulate me on my work, and to invite me to visit them. But I knew him by reputation. He was in every respect one of the most influential citizens in the United States, prestigious and commanding. It was for this reason that I was pleasantly surprised to see a charming and unaffected man come to greet me in colorful shorts and an unbuttoned shirt.

The setting was marvelous. The large white house was typically Cape Cod and stood on a green hill whose gentle slope led to the sea. Boats danced on the water and I could just see a cluster of children prancing on the private white-sand beach.

When I entered the house, I was told that Jack would arrive shortly; he was still in his own home, built on the same property, named "The Enclos." Soon after, Jack appeared. Tall and handsome, his step was loose like an athlete's, but his demeanor was aristocratic. He filled the room. Aside from his uncombed hair, he looked very formal. He wore a blue-striped suit, a white shirt, a tie, and black shoes. Rather unusual for a sunny Sunday on Cape Cod. Although I had hoped for a more relaxed appearance and casual clothes, I understood the seriousness of the subject who stood before me. After all, he was an important senator from a very important state, and the son of Joseph P. Kennedy. I didn't yet know the other Jack Kennedy, the one I was to discover and love.

It turned out that this sitting was to be the first of many and the beginning of a genuine friendship with him and his family. A few months later, JFK asked me to cover his presidential campaign. This was an unforgettable time for me. As soon as he became president of the United States, he asked that I become the official photographer to the White House, the highest position a photographer could hope for. I declined because I didn't want to work for the government, and especially because I wanted to return to New York. I felt I had done enough. But the President asked me to stick around and complete a series on his government. I wouldn't regret it, he assured me. Obviously, he wanted me to stay close, which I did until I finished the project. And like he promised, I didn't regret staying. I never have regretted it.

The year 1999 has just begun, and if he were alive, John Kennedy would turn 80 in May. He was only President for three short years, but today, thirty-five years after his death, he is famous like no other. Everyone, his friends and enemies alike, remember precisely what they were doing the moment they learned of his death. Even children who were too young to understand international affairs have the instant etched in their memories. Perhaps because it was the first time they saw their mother cry, or perhaps because it was the first time they were allowed to watch T.V. for as long as they wanted.

t hose who were not yet born in 1963 also know him because the legend of this murdered hero will always be a part our collective conscience. John Fitzgerald Kennedy was truly a hero. He was young and handsome. His intelligence, his youth, his love of life, and his sense of humor illuminated his government. Americans, and through them, the entire world, were proud of their country; the future seemed to glow despite the somber reality of the Cold War. Even in the Soviet Union, as I would later discover, there was a certain admiration for this American president.

His martyrdom elevated him above simple mortals. There have been so many corrupt figures and tragic events that have come after him that his short reign appears almost perfect, even though some feel his term wasn't particularly distinguished. Lyndon Johnson had the Vietnam War, Nixon had Cambodia and the Watergate scandal; there was the very minor President Ford, the inefficient Jimmy Carter, and today, Clinton is marred by scandal. This all makes us miss President Kennedy even more.

Internationally, the world is in turmoil. The Soviet Union has disappeared, but we don't feel safer for it. And even though leaders everywhere attempt to imitate Kennedy, they can only reproduce his mannerisms or his television appearances. But never his amazing presence. This is why we continue to love him. All of us. For those who had the privilege of knowing him personally, his death was a tragedy that left a gaping hole. I truly believe that none of us has been able to overcome the shock of his death, nor the death of his brother Bobby. Every time a political figure emerges, whether in the United States or elsewhere, we can't help but compare him to Jack Kennedy, whether we want to or not.

I loved him deeply. He has been with me my entire life, and I still feel his influence today. I hope that these photographs will allow the reader to understand why we were so attached to this man who, thirty-five years after his death, continues to guide our lives.

Jacques Lowe, 1999

The New Frontier

(Los Angeles, July 15, 1960: Address of Senator John F. Kennedy accepting the Democratic Party's nomination for the President of the United States.)

But I tell you the New Frontier is here, whether we seek it or not. Beyond that frontier are the uncharted areas of science and space, unsolved problems of peace and war, unconquered pockets of ignorance and prejudice, unanswered questions of poverty and surplus. It would be easier to shrink back from that frontier, to look to the safe mediocrity of the past, to be lulled by good intentions and high rhetoric—and those who prefer that course should not cast their votes for me, regardless of party.

But I believe the times demand new invention, innovation, imagination, decision. I am asking each of you to be pioneers on that New Frontier. My call is to the young in heart, regardless of age—to all who respond to the Scriptural call: "Be strong and of a good courage; be not afraid, neither be thou dismayed."[...] For the harsh facts of the matter are that we stand on this frontier at a turning-point in history. We must prove all over again whether this nation—or any nation so conceived—can long endure—whether our society—with its freedom of choice, its breadth of opportunity, its range of alternatives—can compete with the single-minded advance of the Communist system. [...]

Presidential campaign

(New York, November 5, 1960)

Should I be successful next Tuesday, I want above all else to be a President known [...] as one who not only prevented war but won the peace—as one of whom history might say: he not only laid the foundations for peace in his time, but for generations to come as well. [...] I want to be a President known [...] as one who not only held back the Communist tide but advanced the cause of freedom [...] I have no wish to be known as a narrowly partisan President, or as a private-interest President; I want to be President of all the people. [...] I want to be a President who has the confidence of the people, and who takes the people into his confidence; who lets them know what he is doing and where we are going [...] I want to be a President [...] who is willing to take the responsibility for getting things done, and take the blame if they are not done right. [...]

I want to be a President who recognizes every citizen's rights as well as his obligations [...] a President who cares deeply about the people he represents. [...]

Inaugural address

(Washington, January 20, 1961)

Let every nation know, whether it wishes us well or ill, that we shall pay any price, bear any burden, meet any hardship, support any friend, oppose any foe to assure the survival and the success of liberty.

This much we pledge—and more.

To those old allies whose cultural and spiritual origins we share, we pledge the loyalty of faithful friends. United there is little we cannot do in a host of cooperative ventures. Divided there is little we can do—for we dare not meet a powerful challenge at odds and split asunder.

[...]To those people in the huts and villages of half the globe struggling to break the bonds of mass misery, we pledge our best efforts to help them help themselves, for whatever period is required–not because the communists may be doing it, not because we seek their votes, but because it is right. If a free society cannot help the many who are poor, it cannot save the few who are rich.

[...]But neither can two great and powerful groups of nations take comfort from our present course—both sides overburdened by the cost of modern weapons, both rightly alarmed by the steady spread of the deadly atom, yet both racing to alter that uncertain balance of terror that stays the hand of mankind's final war.

So let us begin anew—remembering on both sides that civility is not a sign of weakness, and sincerity is always subject to proof. Let us never negotiate out of fear. But let us never fear to negotiate.

[...]And if a beachhead of cooperation may push back the jungle of suspicion, let both sides join in creating a new endeavor, not a new balance of power, but a new world of law, where the strong are just and the weak secure and the peace preserved.

[...] And so, my fellow Americans: ask not what your country can do for you–ask what you can do for your country.

My fellow citizens of the world: ask not what America will do for you, but what together we can do for the freedom of man.

From the Soviet threat to Cuba

(Washington, April 20, 1961)

The message of Cuba, of Laos, of the rising din of Communist voices in Asia and Latin America-these messages are all the same. The complacent, the self-indulgent, the soft societies are about to be swept away with the debris of history. Only the strong, only the industrious, only the determined, only the courageous, only the visionary who determine the real nature of our struggle can possibly survive.

No greater task faces this country or this administration. No other challenge is more deserving of our every effort and energy. [...]

We intend to intensify our efforts for a struggle in many ways more difficult than war, where disappointment will often accompany us.

Berlin: the point of confrontation

(Washington, July 25, 1961: Speech delivered at a time when the USSR threatened to sign a separate peace treaty with East Germany, endangering the existence of West Germany.)

In Berlin, as you recall, he intends to bring to an end, through a stroke of the pen, first our legal rights to be in West Berlin—and secondly our ability to make good on our commitment to the two million free people of that city. That we cannot permit.

[…]Berlin is not a part of East Germany, but a separate territory under the control of the allied powers. […]Thus, our presence in West Berlin, and our access thereto, cannot be ended by any act of the Soviet government. The NATO shield was long ago extended to cover West Berlin—and we have given our word that an attack upon that city will be regarded as an attack upon us all.

For West Berlin […]is more than a showcase of liberty, a symbol, an island of freedom in a Communist sea. It is even more than a link with the Free World, a beacon of hope behind the Iron Curtain, an escape hatch for refugees.

West Berlin is all of that. But above all it has now become—as never before—the great testing place of Western courage and will, a focal point where our solemn commitments stretching back over the years since 1945, and Soviet ambitions now meet in basic confrontation.

[…]I hear it said that West Berlin is militarily untenable. And so was Bastogne. And so, in fact, was Stalingrad. Any dangerous spot is tenable if men—brave men—will make it so.

We do not want to fight—but we have fought before. And others in earlier times have made the same dangerous mistake of assuming that the West was too selfish and too soft and too divided to resist invasions of freedom in other lands. Those who threaten to unleash the forces of war on a dispute over West Berlin should recall the words of the ancient philosopher: "A man who causes fear cannot be free from fear."

[…]The world is not deceived by the Communist attempt to label Berlin as a hot-bed of war. There is peace in Berlin today. The source of world trouble and tension is Moscow, not Berlin. And if war begins, it will have begun in Moscow and not Berlin.

For the choice of peace or war is largely theirs, not ours.

[…]In short, while we are ready to defend our interests, we shall also be ready to search for peace—in quiet exploratory talks—in formal or informal meetings. […]

Ich bin ein Berliner

(Berlin, June 26, 1963)

There are many people in the world who really don't understand, or say they don't, what is the great issue between the free world and the Communist world. Let them come to Berlin. There are some who say that communism is the wave of the future. Let them come to Berlin. And there are some who say in Europe and elsewhere we can work with the Communists. Let them come to Berlin. And there are even a few who say that it is true that communism is an evil system, but it permits us to make economic progress. *Lass' sie nach Berlin kommen.* Let them come to Berlin.

Freedom has many difficulties and democracy is not perfect, but we have never had to put a wall up to keep our people in, to prevent them from leaving us.

[...]So let me ask you as I close, to lift your eyes beyond the dangers of today, to the hopes of tomorrow, beyond the freedom merely of this city of Berlin, or your country of Germany, to the advance of freedom everywhere, beyond the wall to the day of peace with justice, beyond yourselves and ourselves to all mankind.

Freedom is indivisible, and when one man is enslaved, all are not free. When all are free, then we can look forward to that day when this city will be joined as one and this country and this great Continent of Europe in a peaceful and hopeful globe. When that day finally comes, as it will, the people of West Berlin can take sober satisfaction in the fact that they were in the front lines for almost two decades.

All free men, wherever they may live, are citizens of Berlin, and, therefore, as a free man, I take pride in the words "Ich bin ein Berliner."

Cuba: a reckless and provocative threat to world peace

(Radio and television report, October 22, 1962:
The Cuban Missile Crisis erupted in October 1962, following
the discovery of a Soviet missile base.)

I call upon Chairman Khrushchev to halt and eliminate this clandestine, reckless and provocative threat to world peace and to stable relations between our two nations. I call upon him further to abandon this course of world domination, and to join in an historic effort to end the perilous arms race and to transform the history of man. He has an opportunity now to move the world back from the abyss of destruction—by returning to his government's own words that it had no need to station missiles outside its own territory, and withdrawing these weapons from Cuba—by refraining from any action which will widen or deepen the present crisis—and then by participating in a search for peaceful and permanent solutions.

[...]The path we have chosen for the present is full of hazards, as all paths are—but it is the one most consistent with our character and courage as a nation and our commitments around the world. The cost of freedom is always high—and Americans have always paid it. [...]

Civil Rights

(June 11, 1963: Radio and television report made after the events in Tuscaloosa, Alabama, where two black students were denied access to the University despite the Federal Court order.)

I hope that every American, regardless of where he lives, will stop and examine his conscience about this and other related incidents. This Nation was founded by men of many nations and backgrounds. It was founded on the principle that all men are created equal, and that the rights of every man are diminished when the rights of one man are threatened.

[...]If an American, because his skin is dark, cannot eat lunch in a restaurant open to the public, if he cannot send his children to the best public school available, if he cannot vote for the public officials who will represent him, if, in short, he cannot enjoy the full and free life which all of us want, then who among us would be content to have the color of his skin changed and stand in his place? Who among us would then be content with the counsels of patience and delay?

One hundred years of delay have passed since President Lincoln freed the slaves, yet their heirs, their grandsons, are not fully free. They are not yet freed from the bonds of injustice. They are not yet freed from social and economic oppression. And this Nation, for all its hopes and all its boasts, will not be fully free until all its citizens are free.

We preach freedom around the world, and we mean it, and we cherish our freedom here at home, but are we to say to the world, and much more importantly, to each other that this is the land of the free except for the Negroes; that we have no second-class citizens except Negroes; that we have no class or caste system, no ghettoes, no master race except with respect to Negroes?

Now the time has come for this Nation to fulfill its promise. [...]

Nuclear Test Ban

(July 26, 1963: Radio and television report made after the signing of a partial ban on nuclear testing by the United States, Great Britain and the USSR.)

Yesterday a shaft of light cut into the darkness. Negotiations were concluded in Moscow on a treaty to ban all nuclear tests in the atmosphere, in outer space, and under water. For the first time, an agreement has been reached on bringing the forces of nuclear destruction under international control—a goal first sought in 1946 when Bernard Baruch presented a comprehensive control plan to the United Nations.

[…]This treaty is not the millennium. It will not resolve all conflicts, or cause the Communists to forego their ambitions, or eliminate the dangers of war. It will not reduce our need for arms or allies or programs of assistance to others. But it is an important first step—a step towards peace—a step towards reason—a step away from war.

[…]But history and our own conscience will judge us harsher if we do not now make every effort to test our hopes by action, and this is the place to begin.

According to the ancient Chinese proverb, "A journey of a thousand miles must begin with a single step."

My fellow Americans, let us take that first step. Let us, if we can, step back from the shadows of war and seek out the way of peace. And if that journey is a thousand miles, or even more, let history record that we, in this land, at this time, took the first step.

For a real and clear-sighted peace

(Washington, American University, June 10, 1963)

I have, therefore, chosen this time and this place to discuss a topic on which ignorance too often abounds and the truth is too rarely perceived—yet it is the most important topic on earth: world peace. What kind of peace do I mean? What kind of peace do we seek? Not a Pax Americana enforced on the world by American weapons of war. Not the peace of the grave or the security of the slave. I am talking about genuine peace, the kind of peace that makes life on earth worth living, the kind that enables men and nations to grow and to hope and to build a better life for their children—not merely peace for Americans but peace for all men and women—not merely peace in our time but peace for all time.

[...] No government or social system is so evil that its people must be considered as lacking in virtue. As Americans, we find communism profoundly repugnant as a negation of personal freedom and dignity. But we can still hail the Russian people for their many achievements—in science and space, in economic and industrial growth, in culture and in acts of courage.

[...]The United States, as the world knows, will never start a war. We do not want a war. We do not now expect a war. This generation of Americans has already had enough—more than enough—of war and hate and oppression. We shall be prepared if others wish it. We shall be alert to try to stop it. But we shall also do our part to build a world of peace where the weak are safe and the strong are just. We are not helpless before that task or hopeless of its success. Confident and unafraid, we labor on—not toward a strategy of annihilation but toward a strategy of peace.

"I have no wish to be known as a narrowly partisan President, or as a private-interest President; I want to be President of all the people."

"If a free society cannot
help the many who are poor,
it cannot save the few
who are rich."

Inaugural address, January 20, 1961

DAN'S FRUIT SHOP
STANDARD MARKET
GARDNER AUTO TOP Co
SEAT COVERS
two great Democrats

A TIME FOR GREATNESS
THE JOHN F. KENNEDY STORY

KENNEDY
FOR
PRESIDENT

Oregon Primary May 20, 1960

"And so, my fellow Americans: ask not what your country can do for you—ask what you can do for your country."

"United there is little we cannot do in a host of cooperative ventures. Divided there is little we can do—for we dare not meet a powerful challenge at odds and split asunder."

Inaugural address, January 20, 1961

"But are we to say to the world [...] that this is the land of the free except for the Negroes; [...] Now the time has come for this Nation to fulfill its promise."

Civil Rights, June 11, 1963

"Let us never negotiate out of fear.
But let us never fear to negotiate."

Inaugural address, January 20, 1961

"And this Nation, for all its hopes and all its boasts, will not be fully free until all its citizens are free."

"The cost of freedom is always high—and
Americans have always paid it."

October 22, 1962

JUNE 1964
PRICE 60c
GREAT BRITAIN 4/6

Esquire

THE MAGAZINE FOR MEN

Kennedy without tears.
See page 108.

Chronology

c. 1850: Patrick Kennedy, great-grandfather of John Fitzgerald, immigrates from Ireland and settles in Boston.

1914: Joseph Kennedy marries Rose Fitzgerald, daughter of the mayor of Boston.

1917: On May 29, in Brookline, Massachusetts, John Fitzgerald Kennedy is born, the second son of Joseph and Rose.

1936: John F. Kennedy enters Harvard.

1937: In the summer, he travels to Europe (France, Italy and Spain).

1938: Joseph Kennedy is appointed Ambassador to the United States in London.

1939: John F. Kennedy travels again to the European continent, this time to France, Poland, USSR, Turkey and the Balkans.

1940: John F. Kennedy publishes *Why England Slept*, an essay on English political life before Churchill.

1941: He is discharged due to a wounded spine. In December, after five months of back rehabilitation, he is able to join the Marines.

1942: In August, Lieutenant Kennedy's patrol boat sinks in the Solomon Islands.

1943: On August 2, John's older brother, Joseph Kennedy Junior, is killed in an air battle in Europe.

1945-46: John F. Kennedy tries his hand at journalism. Travels to Latin America.
In November 1946, he is reelected as representative of Massachusetts, to the district of Boston. He would be elected again in 1948 and 1950.
In December, the first Indochina War begins.

1948: In November, Harry Truman is elected president of the United States.

1949: In April, NATO is founded.
In August-September, the Federal Republic of Germany is founded.
In October, the People's Republic of China and the Democratic Republic of Germany are born.

1950: In June, the Korean War begins.

1952: Dwight Eisenhower is elected president of the United States.
In November, John Kennedy is elected senator of Massachusetts.

1953: In March, Stalin dies. Khrushchev becomes first secretary of the Soviet Communist Party.
In June, Ethel and Julius Rosenberg are executed in the United States, accused of espionage.
In July, armistice in Korea.
In September, John F. Kennedy marries Jacqueline Bouvier.

1954: The American nuclear submarine, *The Nautilus*, is launched.
In May, fall of Dien Bien Phu.
On May 17, the Supreme Court of the United States declares racial segregation in public schools unconstitutional.
In July, the armistice is signed in Indochina.
In September, Mao Tse-Tung becomes president of the People's Republic of China.
In October, West Germany is allowed by the London conference to rearm. West Germany enters NATO.
In November, John F. Kennedy undergoes a spinal operation.

1955: John F. Kennedy publishes *Profiles in Courage.*
In May, once he is healed, he returns to the Senate.

1956: John F. Kennedy supports the Democratic presidential candidate Adlai Stevenson. He is not nominated vice president by the Democratic Party. Eisenhower is reelected president of the United States.

1957: In October, the first Soviet *Sputnik* is launched.

1958: In January, Polaris, the first American missile is launched.
On June 1, in France, General de Gaulle becomes head of the government.
In November, John F. Kennedy is reelected senator of Massachusetts. General de Gaulle is elected president of the French Republic.

1959: In January, the European Economic Community comes into force.
In September, a Soviet spaceship reaches the moon.
Khrushchev visits the United States.

1960: In January, John F. Kennedy officially announces his candidacy for president of the United States.
In March, Khrushchev visits France.
In April, Charles de Gaulle visits the United States.
In July, the Democratic party elects John F. Kennedy as its candidate for president.
In August, Fidel Castro nationalizes American companies in Cuba.
On November 8, JFK is elected president of the United States. He wins by the smallest margin since 1884 (49.7 % against 49.6 % for Richard Nixon). He is the first Catholic president in the history of the country.

1961: On January 4, diplomatic relations between Cuba and the United States rupture.
On January 20, President Kennedy assumes his office.
In April, the Soviet Gagarin becomes the first man to go into space.
On April 17, the Bay of Pigs invasion in Cuba.
In May, the first American goes into space.
In May-June, Kennedy meets with Charles de Gaulle in Paris.
Early June, Kennedy meets with Khrushchev in Vienna.
In August, the Soviet astronaut Titov circles the earth seventeen times. The Berlin wall is built.
On August 30, the USSR ends the nuclear moratorium.
On September 1, the Soviets perform nuclear tests in space.
On September 15, the United States begins underground nuclear testing.

1962: On April 25, the United States performs nuclear testing in space.
In October, the Cuban missile crisis. The USSR removes its missiles from Cuba.

1963: In May, racial incidents in Birmingham, Alabama.
On June 20, the "red telephone" hotline is established between Washington and Moscow.
In June-July, Kennedy travels to Europe (Federal Republic of Germany, West Berlin, Ireland, Great Britain, Italy).
On July 25, the Limited Test Ban Treaty is signed.
On August 28, the great march on Washington. Martin Luther King delivers his famous "I have a dream" speech.
On November 22, John F. Kennedy is assassinated in Dallas. Lyndon Johnson becomes president of the United States.

The Soviet delegation in front of the president's coffin:
Anastas Mikoyan and Anatoly Dobrynin, ambassadors to the Soviet Union in Washington.

JFK

During the war, in Charleston, South Carolina. Discharged because of a wounded back from which he would suffer his whole life, John Kennedy goes through five months of physical therapy in order to be able to join the Marines in December 1941. Courtesy the Kennedy family and the John Fitzgerald Kennedy Library. © All Rights reserved

The Solomon Islands, where Lieutenant Kennedy is posted during the war. In August 1942, his patrol boat sinks. Courtesy the Kennedy family and the John Fitzgerald Kennedy Library. © All Rights reserved
Senator Kennedy leaving his Georgetown home at 3307 N Street for Congress. Spring 1959. Jackie at his side. They marry in 1953 and Caroline is born in 1957.

John F. Kennedy arrives in Portland, Oregon for a meeting, early 1960. At this time, the senator is still only a primary candidate for presidential nomination. Only a few months later, airports would be filled with supporters. In 1961, once President, Kennedy would tell Jacques Lowe that this campaign photograph was his favorite; "No one remembers this time anymore."

On the campaign trail, during the West Virginia primaries, March 1960. John F. Kennedy, in his airplane-turned-headquarters, on his way to Charleston. Cuban cigars soon become part of the future president's image. During the Cuban Missile Crisis and the American embargo (1962), a rumor would circulate that John F. Kennedy had stocked up on enough of these famous cigars to hold him over for the necessary amount of time.

Wisconsin, fall 1960. Jacques Lowe took the portrait of JFK displayed behind him during their very first meeting in July 1958.

Alone at the beginning of the Presidential Campaign, Oregon, fall 1959. Breakfast with Jackie and Steve Smith, a member of the election team. In the early days of the campaign, few came to hear the message of the senator who wanted to "get the country moving again."

An ever-more insistent crowd. In a display usually reserved for rock stars and not for politicians, some of John F. Kennedy's supporters became hysterical. Some young women remained speechless and frozen, crying and shaking, while others shouted out their enthusiasm.

First campaign poster. Primaries, Oregon, May 20, 1960.
Omaha, Nebraska, summer 1959. Photograph taken during one of the first stops covered by Lowe. Nothing out of the ordinary has been scheduled, but the candidate's charisma quickly energizes the scene. This photograph would soon be used for his campaign (see opposite page) and term. After his assassination, the image would appear on stamps.

In search of voices, 1960. Between Parkersburg and Charleston, John F. Kennedy meets a group of students with their teachers. He stops the car and gets onto a tractor to mobilize the young Democratic vote.
New place, new words, same message. Rally, 1960.

John and Robert Kennedy, Biltmore Hotel, Los Angeles, July 14, 1960, the night before the Democratic nomination. Robert F. Kennedy, JFK's most adamant supporter (JFK would appoint him Attorney General), would never really accept the decision to name Lyndon Johnson vice president. JFK's choice proved to be a good one, since it won him Texas. Without this crucial state, he could have lost the elections.

The power of conviction in Kennedy's speeches, 1960. On the campaign trail, sleeping and eating does not figure into the candidate and his team's schedule. Shortly before the elections, arriving at the crack of dawn in a city after marathon days, he would always find his next audience, a crowd of several thousand shouting, "We love you, Jack! We love you, Jack!"

Three Kennedy women: Eunice Kennedy Shriver, sister of the candidate, Joan Bennett Kennedy, Edward's wife, and Ethel Skakel Kennedy, Robert's wife, in Los Angeles, July 15, 1960. The delegates for the Democratic Party have just named John F. Kennedy their candidate for president.
Robert and his wife Ethel in the polling booth, November 8, 1960. Presidential elections. JFK is elected president, defeating Republican Richard Nixon.

77

Head to head, Richard Nixon/John F. Kennedy, first televised debate of the campaign, New York, September 26, 1960. A comfortable, at ease Kennedy faces a nervous and sweating Nixon who accuses him of being too inexperienced. Kennedy comes out of this televised confrontation a winner. After, his face would become as well-known as that of his Republican rival.

Listening to the results, at the home of Robert Kennedy, Hyannis Port, November 9, 1960. JFK surrounded by family and campaign workers (including Pierre Salinger, the president's future Press Secretary, second from the right), eyes glued to the television, listening to the results being announced live. At this moment, Illinois and Minnesota's votes have not yet been announced. Not even an hour after this photograph was taken, Kennedy was announced president of the United States.

Joy all around at the Democratic Convention, Los Angeles, July 16, 1960. The battle for the vice presidency is already in full force in the adjacent room at the Biltmore Hotel.

Rally in Kansas, fall 1960.
July 15, 1960, in front of more than 100,000 people. Kennedy, just declared the Democratic candidate, delivers his speech on the New Frontier (social justice, the resolution of racial problems, and the conquest of space). Los Angeles Coliseum.

"Now my wife and I are preparing for a new administration and a new baby." On November 25, 1960, Jackie Kennedy gives birth to John Fitzgerald Junior, brother of Caroline, born three years earlier.

Senator Lyndon Johnson, Robert and John Kennedy, a few moments before the official announcement of his nomination for vice president. Los Angeles, July, 1960.

In London, at the home of his sister-in-law, Lee Radziwill, with his Press Secretary Pierre Salinger. Reading the press's comments on his recent meeting with Khrushchev in Vienna, June 1961. Khrushchev had underestimated the young president, and threatened to take over West Berlin during the meeting. He was more pleasant about Jackie, telling journalists that he wanted a picture of her and Kennedy; "I would rather shake her hand…" On the Caroline, September 1959.

In front of the Tomb of the Unknown Soldier, at the side of Charles de Gaulle, Paris, June, 1961. First official trip abroad for the American presidential couple. JFK would then travel to Vienna to meet Nikita Khrushchev.

January 20, 1961, presidential inauguration, John F. Kennedy leaves his Georgetown home to head into the city. To his right, the official procession of cars to the Capitol, where the new President takes oath. In the limousines are Dwight Eisenhower and his vice president Richard Nixon, John F. Kennedy and his vice president Lyndon Johnson, and their wives.

Kennedy meets with his advisers, January 25, 1961. The subject is Fidel Castro. The prime minister of Cuba since 1959, he would adopt the Communist doctrine in 1962. His relationship with the Soviet Union provoked and threatened the United States.

Telephone conversation with Adlai Stevenson, American ambassador to the United Nations, February 13, 1961. At this moment, Kennedy has learned of the assassination of Patrice Lumumba, prime minister of the Congo. As senator, Kennedy was convinced that the United States needed to establish its intentions with Africa. The continent was in the process of decolonization and on the brink of choosing between Western and Soviet models of government.

In the Oval Office, May 1961.

Impatient and in a hurry, Kennedy preferred to dictate his speeches into a Dictaphone rather than use the services of a secretary. He often spent hours at the end of the day doing so. He would find his notes typed up on his desk the following day. In Coos Bay, Oregon, end of 1959. Jacques Lowe remembers never having seen the future president doubt his powers of conviction to such an extent as after addressing a very hostile group of fishermen.

"President Kennedy died a soldier, under fire, serving his duty and his country." (Charles de Gaulle)
"The loss for the United States and for the world is incalculable. Those who succeed him must fight even harder to attain the ideals of world peace, of happiness and of dignity of mankind to which he devoted his term." (Winston Churchill)

The publisher would like to thank
Jacques Lowe and Thomasina Lowe for their help.
Thanks are also due to
Esquire Magazine and to the John Fitzgerald Kennedy Library.